Roman Silbury
and the
Harvest Goddess

Michael Dames

Heart of Albion

Roman Silbury and the Harvest Goddess

Michael Dames

Front cover:
Top: Ceres, Roman goddess of Harvest, with sickle, and wheat ears (Corinium Museum, Cirencester).
Bottom: Wheat field, north side of Silbury, late July, 2006.

ISBN 978-1-905646-06-7

Published by
Heart of Albion Press
2 Cross Hill Close, Wymeswold
Loughborough, LE12 6UJ

albion@indigogroup.co.uk

Visit our Web site: www.hoap.co.uk

Printed in England

Roman Silbury and the Harvest Goddess

In AD 50 the invading Romans first set eyes on Silbury Hill, Europe's tallest prehistoric monument. By then it was 2,500 years old. Yet it gripped the Roman imagination, as Roman ritual shafts, rediscovered nearby in the twentieth century, clearly show. The major Roman settlement, detected in 2007 at the eastern foot of Silbury, confirms their keen interest in the site.

Dr Bob Bewley, Regional Director of English Heritage, believes that the Romans were 'drawn in the wake of their prehistoric forebears' by a sense of sacred value, expressed through pilgrimage to the monument. Granted such continuity, did the Neolithic and Roman worship at Silbury address a shared issue? If so, what?

Perhaps harvest. Agriculture was brought to Britain before 3,000 BC, and Britain's corn-growing power helped to draw the Romans here. An ear of barley appears on British king Cunobelin's gold coins, while Roman coins of AD 45 showed an image of the corn goddess Ceres. As I suggest in *The Silbury Treasure* (published 1976), the need for grain inspired the building of Silbury, and might explain its relevance to the Romans.

But the immense effort required to build Silbury renders it an absurdity in practical farming terms. So we must look beneath mundane sense, to eras where wheat and barley were regarded as gifts from the gods. This conviction was held in Neolithic and Roman Britain. Therefore Silbury Hill, together with its surrounding lake, could still be seen as a vast 1140 feet long image of the enduring, pregnant harvest goddess.

Drawn on an architectural scale, Silbury Hill and its carefully designed 'moat' were, I argued in *The Silbury Treasure,* planned from the outset to describe the pregnant harvest goddess in superhuman form. With the help of sun and moonlight, playing on her water body, she repeatedly gave birth to a divine 'harvest child', seen also in the sacred corn crop, grown annually on the flat summit of her 130 feet high 'womb'-hill.

As regards the overall shape of the Silbury effigy, innumerable Neolithic figurines depict the goddess of agriculture in a similar mode, squatting in 'childbirth'.

a

b

c

Three views of The Harvest Goddess

a: Seen from her water head, towards her pregnant womb

b: Across her breast

c: Over her thigh, to the Roman settlement site, marked [R].

a

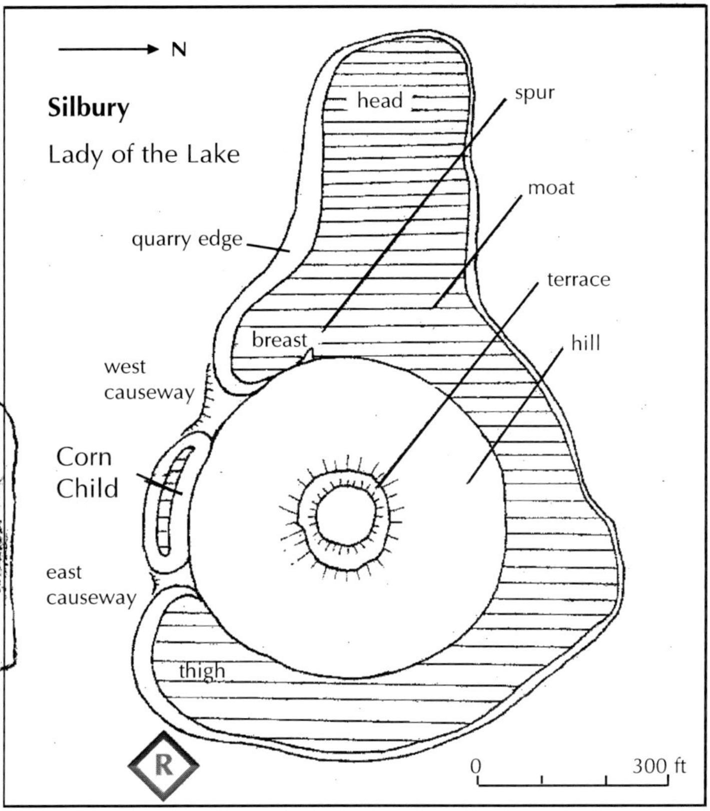

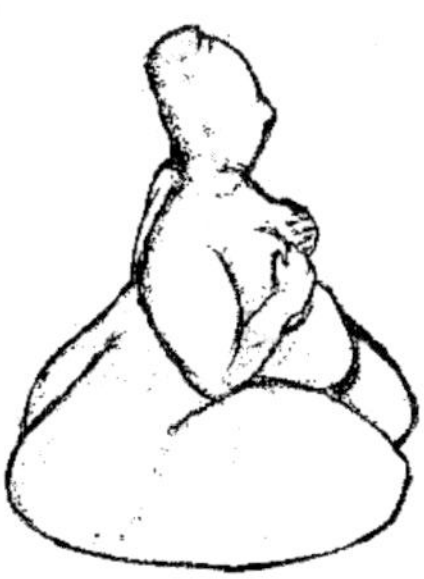

b

c

d

a: Dea Nutrix, Roman Mother goddess, suckling twins, second century AD, Canterbury, 15 cm high.

b: Squatting goddess figurine, Catal Huyuk, Anatolia, circa 6,000 BC. Similar images to this are found in many parts of Neolithic Eurasia.

c: Britain as Britannia; Roman coin of Antoninus Pius, AD 140–4. When the whole island was accepted as a superhuman female, the vast scale of the Silbury effigy presented no difficulty to Romans.

d: Goddess, Pazardzik, Bulgaria, 4,000 BC.

a: Ceres, Roman goddess of agriculture. Intaglio brooch from Holt, Denbyshire. She offers corn ears and a dish of fruit over an altar. Dozens of Roman brooches engraved with Ceres' image have been found in Britain.

b: Ceres, reverse of Claudius' coin, mid-first century AD, minted in Roman Corinium (Cirencester).

c: Barley head, on reverse of Cunobelin's gold stater. He was a British king of the Atrebates, early first century AD.

d: Bronze figurine of Ceres (Greek Demeter), carrying torches. Water Newton, Huntingdonshire.

e: Ceres-Demeter hands ears of corn and knowledge of ploughing to Triptolemus for world wide distribution. Roman mosaic, Brading, Isle of Wight.

f: Tellus Mater, Roman 'Mother Earth', with a corn measure vessel on her head. Lost Roman mosaic, Newton St Loe, Somerset.

g: Crowned Ceres with corn ears and dolphins. Roman mosaic, Nunney, Somerset.

The incoming Romans were always notably willing to merge their own deities with the closest equivalents they could find in the countries that they occupied. They probably saw in the Neolithic 'Lake goddess' (who we call Silbury) their own goddess of agriculture, named Ceres. So Ceres merged with Britain's prehistoric deity.

As in human pregnancy, the material for the Neolithic chalk 'womb' and stylized creation mound was drawn from the 'quarry' that became the mother's still-visible watery body. Two 'causeways' of undisturbed chalk, left *in situ* by the designers, define her 200 feet long 'harvest child'. It was born when the full moon closest to the August 1st, (the solar quarter day, Christianised as Lammas, 'loaf mass'), re-animated her water body from thigh to breast. Then the hilltop sacred wheat could be cut as part of the first fruits birth process, following which general harvest might start across prehistoric Britain. (See *The Silbury Treasure*, chapters 4, 6, and 12).

Despite clogging of her moat by recent silt, the Silbury rock and water goddess remains visible for much of each year, more or less in her original form. Her curvaceous body can be seen by walking the periphery, although the Neolithic viewing terrace, just below the summit, is now out of bounds.

Ceres in Roman literature

Just as Roman art confirms a continuity of devotion to Silbury, the grandest expression of the eternal harvest goddess in prehistoric Britain, so Roman writings help voice illiterate prehistory's reverence for that deity, whatever she was called.

Ovid's *Fasti* of the late first century BC lists Tellus' and Ceres' festivals, beginning in January, and suggesting their joint adoration throughout the year:

> When the seed has been sown and the field fertilised... propitiate Earth and Ceres, the mothers of the corn, with their own spelt [a primitive mountain wheat, also known to the Saxons], and flesh of teeming sow'. In Neolithic Europe and later, the Earth was often identified with the female pig. [Pigs' bones were found in a Roman shaft near Silbury].

Ceres' name derives from the root *ker-*, 'growth'. Ovid prays to Ceres: 'O satisfy the eager husbandmen with boundless crops, that they may reap the due reward of their tillage. O grant unto the tender seeds unbroken increase... when the seed is buried, sprinkle it with water from the skies.'

Top: *Tellus; low relief from Carthage; now in the Louvre, Paris. Embedded in the rock that she represents, and with Neptune lapping at her feet, she nurtures human infants, sheep, cattle, storks, snakes and vegetation. A spring gushes from her urn.*
Bottom: *Tellus Mater, Altar of Peace, Rome, circa 10 BC. Here her close connection with Air (left) and Water (right) is emphasised.*

Demeter-Ceres, with corn, poppies and snakes; terracotta, Terme museum, Rome.

He begs the goddesses to ward off attacks by birds, ants, mildew, blight and weeds before asking the farmers to repeat these prayers.

He ends by praising Ceres as a goddess of Peace, a role that she probably inherited from the relatively unwarlike Neolithic: 'Under your foot long time war has been laid in chains... Peace is the nurse of Ceres, and Ceres is the foster-child of Peace', he affirms.

At the *Cerealia* festival, held annually on 19th April, Ceres was again honoured, for 'her bounty and services are manifest'. These 'Games of Ceres' involved offerings of 'spurting salt and incense [if available] and the waving of 'resinous torches'. In Rome in 484 BC, the first bronze sculpture ever cast was of Ceres, and placed in her temple near the Aventine, where the grain ships moored. As in rural Britannia, it was the common people (the Plebs of Rome) who were especially devoted to her.

In Virgil's *Aeneid*, composed late first century BC, Ceres plays a vital role in Rome's birth. On fleeing a burning Troy, the demi-god Aeneas gathers the fugitives together on 'a hillock with an ancient and deserted shrine of Ceres.' When eventually he and his followers, as prophesised, make

William Stukeley's drawing, shows Silbury in the upper Kennet valley. That river's source is the Swallowhead spring, shown [S]. The Winterbourne tributary [centre], flows passed the Avebury Henge monument and Silbury's east side. The recently-discovered Roman settlement is shown [R].

landfall near the Tiber's mouth, they sit down to eat on a 'flooring provided by Ceres', namely grass (proto corn). The only plates at this first feast are Ceres' 'meal cakes, thin cereal platters', regarded as 'the round-shaped crust of destiny', which they eat. Thus before Rome can be founded, the goddess of agriculture is first recognised as vital to its survival. All cities depend on Ceres' food.

Because of the warmer climate in Italy, Ceres' wheat was ready to be cut by 15th June, when the *penus Vestae*, or symbolic grain store of the Roman state had been purified to receive the sacred First Fruits; and on 25th August the Latin goddess Ops Consiva, 'Abundance personified', was celebrated. She presided over the fully garnered crops.

Tellus and Ceres

Ceres and Tellus (or Earth) are 'Partners in labour and discharge a common function,' writes Ovid. Thus the April Cerialia was paired with, and preceded by, the 15th April Fordicidia festival of Tellus, at which a pregnant cow was sacrificed. Tellus was the 'ground mother' in whom Ceres, the mistress of farming processes, operated. Tellus was the place, the foundation that sustained every sacred imagining, a deity set to outlast all human constructs. She may be sensed around Silbury in the

a

b

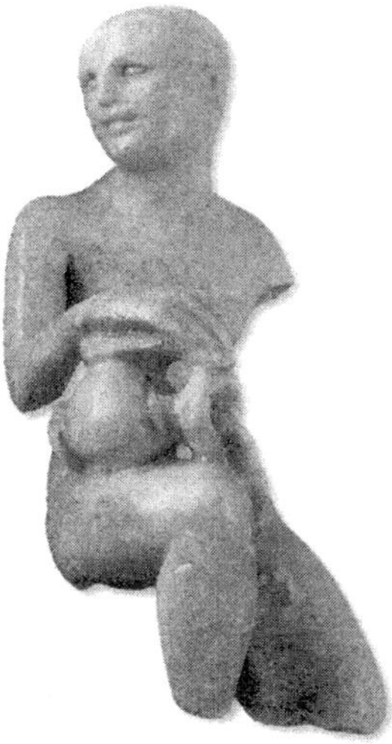

c

a: Swallowhead stream, birth of the River Kennet.
b: Roman water nymphs, from Woodchester villa, Gloucestershire, fourth century AD.
c: Water nymph with jug; bone, 4 cm high; Corinium Museum, Cirencester.

neighbouring hills and streams, that were venerated by both Romans and Stone Age peoples.

Among the many dry valleys of the chalk Marlborough Downs, the copious and beautiful Swallowhead spring, traditionally regarded as the Roiver Kennet's birthplace, has been a notably animated exception. This spring is much older than humanity.

In both *The Silbury Treasure* and *The Avebury Cycle*, I argue that Swallowhead became *the* sacred focus for early Neolithic veneration in the district, and then inspired the monuments built around its pure water suource during the fourth and third millennia BC. There a holy stream-child of 'Mother Earth' is repeatedly born to the surface. To this day, on visiting the spot, people are touched by the gift.

Naiads or water nymphs are young female divinities that haunt healing springs. Daughters of river deities, they are benevolent guardian spirits of

Reconstructed nymphaeum at Roman Vindolanda, Northumberland, with interior view.

pure water sources such as Swallowhead, which retained its reputation for curative herbs beyond 1800.

Swallowhead water was drunk on the Silbury summit on Mothering Sunday till 1853.

Roman nymphs are a Classical version of local springhead spirits of place, abounding in prehistoric Britain since the Stone Age, and well-known to the Iron Age inhabitants. An impervious layer of clay creates the Swallowhead spring. The same natural clay layer floors and keeps the water in the Silbury moat (see *The Silbury Treasure* chapter 7).

Opposite:

a: *The Kelpie, a nymph, painted by H. C. Draper, 1913.*

b: *The Romano-British goddess Coventina, holding palm; a stream runs from her vase.*

c: *Coventina's three nymphs, all from Broclatia, Northumburland.*

d: *Nymphaeum at Chedworth Roman villa, Gloucestershire. The spring still flows.*

a
b
c
d

Mother and child at Swallowhead: Tellus' and human life-streams merge.

a and b: Pregnant Silbury rises over the foreground Swallowhead gully.
c: Mother goddesses with infant, bread and fruit; Roman, Corinium Museum, Cirencester.

a

b

c

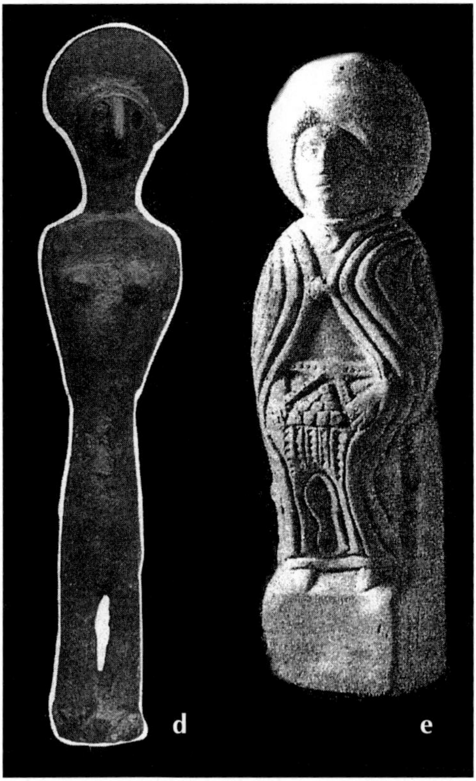

Nocturnal torchlight processions were involved in Ceres' worship: 'And thou, Ceres, in whose honour we, your silent priests, ever brandish the votive torch, as we hurry on our panting course'. (Statius, *Silvar, 4)*

Deae Suli at Bath

a: *Head of Luna, the Roman moon goddess, temple at Aquae Sulis, Bath.*

b: *Hot spring, Bath.*

c: *Altar to Sul, goddess of the hot spring. Sul's worship extended to Solsbury Hill, overlooking Bath. At full moon, the Luna-Sul duo may have re-enacted the August birth ritual on that hill, so replicating the Swallowhead-Silbury event (see* The Silbury Treasure *chapter 12).*
The role of the moon at birth nights, emphasised in folklore, is indicated by:

d: *Moon deity, bronze figurine, circa 500 BC; 15cm. high, from Aust Cliff, Gloucestershire. The Welsh First Fruits feast, Gwyl Awst , 'August Vigil', was nocturnal. Welsh* gwyl *derives from Latin* vigil.

e: *'Lunar' Roman goddess with loaves in birth chair; Arrington, Cambridgeshire; pipe clay, 19 cm high.*

The myth of Demeter and Persephone

The Romans brought to Britain the myth of the mother goddess Demeter (alias Ceres) and her daughter Persephone (alias Proserpina). Their story closely matches the divine annual drama described by, and enacted at Silbury and the other Neolithic Avebury monuments (see *The Avebury Cycle,* Michael Dames, 1977; 2nd edn 1996).

a: *Mother Earth corn dolly (idol) from Lower Sands Farm, near Avebury, 1975.*
b: *Demeter greets her abducted daughter returning from Hades. Eleusis, fifth century BC.*
c: *Demeter with Zeus as bull, Persephone's father. Littlecote Park mosaic, Wiltshire, fourth century.*

Opposite:
d: *Demeter as 'winter' mourns the loss of her daughter to the Underworld. Roman mosaic, Bignor, Sussex. Six Roman emperors, including Hadrian,were initiates at Demeter's sanctuary at Eleusis.*

d e

f

g

h

e: *West Kennet chambered long barrow, entrance to the Neolithic Underworld, drawn by William Stukeley.*

f: *Persephone waves goodbye to Demeter. Littlecote Park mosaic, Wiltshire, fourth century.*

g: *Winter as a hooded boy, Chedworth villa mosaic, Gloucestershire.*

h: *Persephone, with her underworld husband, Hades. Greek, ceramic, third century BC.*

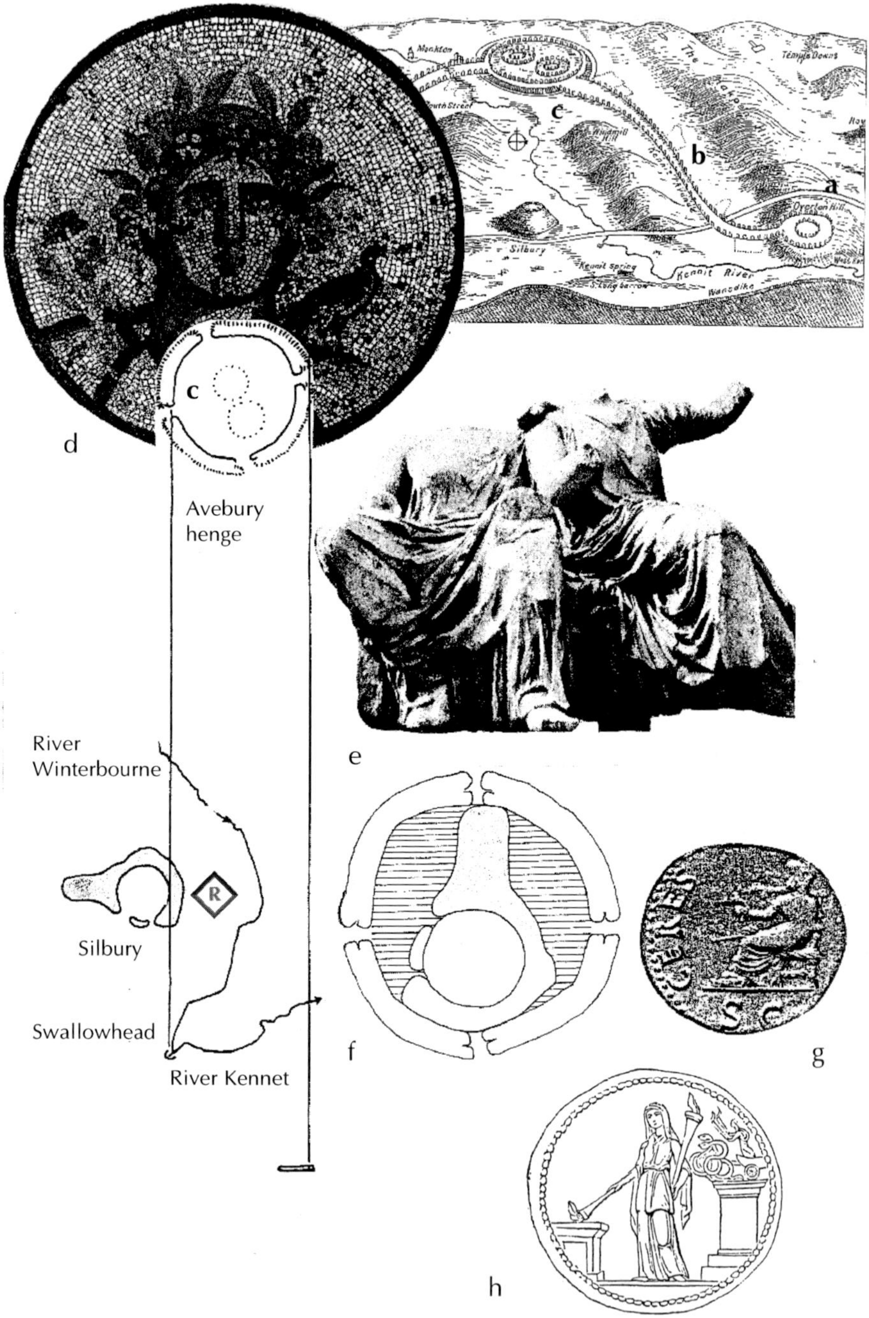
a
b
c
Silbury
Overton Hill
c
d
Avebury
henge
e
River
Winterbourne
Silbury
Swallowhead
River Kennet
f
CERES
S C
g
h

Roman myth and the Neolithic monument

Proserpina, epitome of springtime, is picking flowers in a meadow when the ground gives way and she is captured by Hades, ruler of the Underworld. Her mother, says Ovid, then 'kindled two pine trees' as torches. She searches for Proserpina by night and day, through air and over ocean, with a pair of serpents to pull her chariot. Failing to find her daughter, Ceres decrees that there will be perpetual famine on Earth until she is returned. But Proserpina has *married* Hades (alias Pluto), and cannot desert him. Then Zeus (alias Jupiter) decrees that she shall come back for nine months of every year, and only spend each winter with Hades. There *will* be more harvests, after all. Thus, through their dramas, deities create the seasons as experienced by humanity.

In essence, Ceres' myth is as old as the Neolithic. It enabled the Romans to participate in the annually re-staged cyclical drama, act by act, at the seasonally appropriate Neolithic monuments, arranged around the Swallowhead spring (Roman coin offerings have been found at West Kennet long barrow). For them, as for native British farmers, the similarities with Classical myth were clear. So the newcomers honoured the Neolithic framework and built their pilgrimage settlement at Silbury's foot.

As during the Neolithic, in Roman myth the Daughter-Mother-Death hag modes of the goddess were essentially aspects of one deity, just as the four elements and seasons make a dynamic, unified whole. Thus the Silbury moat length fits exactly across Avebury's henge arena, while each noonday sunbeam links the three major monuments and Swallowhead spring together in a repeatable drama.

a: The Neolithic 'Sanctuary', Overton Hill, drawn by William Stukeley.
b: Snakes, as icons of the reviving life force, take monumental form in the West Kennet and Beckhampton stone avenues.
c: The Avebury henge 'May wedding ring'. The recently-discovered Roman settlement is shown as [R].
d: Proserpina as 'Spring', with flowers and swallow; from The Seasons pavement, fourth century AD, Corinium (Cirencester).
e: Demeter and Persephone; Parthenon, Athens, east pediment, fifth century BC.
f: Silbury, the pregnant mother, aligns due east-west.
g: Ceres enthroned, carrying corn ears; Romano-British coin.
h: Ceres lights her torches and drives her snake chariot; Roman brass medallion of Antoninus Pius, second century AD.

Top: *Mother, daughter and sheaves of oats, Lleyn, Wales, August 1971.*

Bottom: *Man and woman harvesting; fifteenth century misericord, St Mary's, Ripple, Worcestershire. Much medieval pottery has been found embedded in Silbury's top terrace.*

Also by Micchael Dames from Heart of Albion

Taliesin's Travels

A demi-god at large

Michael Dames

Taliesin's Travels brings fresh significance to one of Britain's best-loved tales.

For over a thousand years the impish Taliesin has enthralled and enlightened people. As a farmer's son, he is grounded in the land. Yet, because his mother is the goddess Nature, he can travel, free as a demi-god, throughout time and space.

Thanks to his intimate contact with spirits of place, sun and underworld, Taliesin reveals and portrays the interconnecting, ever-transforming essence of life. His often painful and sometimes ludicrous adventures engage with creation in its entirety. Transcending history, he invites us to see our own millennium as a cyclical, mythic journey so that, like him, each individual comes to identify with the whole of creation.

With a keen sense of enjoyment, Michael Dames provides a deep and imaginative account of the tales and poetry associated with Taliesin. Prehistoric, Romano-British and Christian aspects of Taliesin's persona are brought together in a magical synthesis.

Michael Dames is well-known for his pioneering studies of the myths and legends of the British Isles. His previous books include *The Silbury Treasure, The Avebury Cycle, Mythic Ireland* and *Merlin and Wales.*

EAN 978 1872 883 892. ISBN 1 872883 89 3. Published 2006.
245 x 175 mm, over 200 illustrations, paperback
£16.95

Heart of Albion

The UK's leading publisher of
folklore, mythology and cultural studies.

Further details of all Heart of Albion titles online at
www.hoap.co.uk

To order books or request our current catalogue
please contact

Heart of Albion Press

2 Cross Hill Close, Wymeswold

Loughborough, LE12 6UJ

Phone: 01509 880725

Fax: 01509 881715

email: albion@indigogroup.co.uk

Web site: www.hoap.co.uk